Y0-BZF-860

ENGINEERING
Entrepreneurs

Heather C. Hudak

CRABTREE
PUBLISHING COMPANY
WWW.CRABTREEBOOKS.COM

Author: Heather C. Hudak

Editors: Sarah Eason, Nancy Dickmann,
Wendy Scavuzzo, and Petrice Custance

Proofreader and indexer: Wendy Scavuzzo

Editorial director: Kathy Middleton

Design: Clare Webber

Cover design and additional artwork: Clare Webber

Photo research: Rachel Blount

**Production coordinator and
Prepress technician:** Tammy McGarr

Print coordinator: Katherine Berti

Consultant: David Hawksett

Produced for Crabtree Publishing Company by Calcium Creative

Photo Credits:

t=Top, tr=Top Right, tl=Top Left

Inside: Blue Frog Robotics: pp. 20, 21; Cast Connex: pp. 12l, 12r, 13b;
© KONE Corporation: p. 11b; Susmita Mohanty: Siddharth Das:
p. 25; Image Credit: Liquifer Systems Group (LSG), Visualisation
Credit: René Waclavicek: p. 24; Newlight Technologies, Inc.: pp. 16c,
17; Nexus-e-water: Josh Fuller: p. 15b; Paper Clip Design Ltd.: p. 23t;
Shutterstock: 3dshtamp: p. 11t; Andrey Armyagov: p. 23b; DGLimages:
pp. 1, 27b; Everett Historical: p. 18r; FrameStockFootages: p. 27t;
Golubovystock: p. 9; Jakkapan: p. 6b; Georgios Kollidas: p. 10; Susan
Santa Maria: p. 16b; Gilles Paire: p. 5t; Quality Stock Arts: p. 18l; SFIO
CRACHO: p. 19t; Syda Productions: p. 7t; Terrctr: p. 15t; TierneyMJ: p.
14; TinnaPong: p. 29; Yakobchuk Viacheslav: p. 8; Andrea Willmore:
p. 28; Olena Yakobchuk: p. 26; Anutr Yossundara: p. 4; Stanford
University: Frederic Osada and Teddy Seguin, DRASSM/Stanford
University: p. 19b; Wikimedia Commons: Mathew Brady: p. 5b; Gina
Collecchia: p. 7b; Claude-Louis Desrais: pp. 3, 22; Levin C. Handy: p.
6t; Prioryman: p. 14b; UN Photo/Logan Abassi UNDP Global: p. 13t.

Cover: Shutterstock: Andrey Popov.

Library and Archives Canada Cataloguing in Publication

Hudak, Heather C., 1975-, author
    Engineering entrepreneurs / Heather Hudak.

(Science and technology start-up stars)
Includes index.
Issued in print and electronic formats.
ISBN 978-0-7787-4412-2 (hardcover).--
ISBN 978-0-7787-4425-2 (softcover).--
ISBN 978-1-4271-2023-6 (HTML)

    1. Engineering--Technological innovations--Juvenile literature.
2. Entrepreneurship--Juvenile literature. I. Title.

TA149.H83 2018   j620   C2017-907656-6
                                      C2017-907657-4

Library of Congress Cataloging-in-Publication Data

CIP available at the Library of Congress

Crabtree Publishing Company

www.crabtreebooks.com   1-800-387-7650

Printed in the U.S.A./022018/CG20171220

**Published in Canada
Crabtree Publishing**
616 Welland Ave.
St. Catharines, Ontario
L2M 5V6

**Published in the United States
Crabtree Publishing**
PMB 59051
350 Fifth Avenue, 59th Floor
New York, New York 10118

**Published in the United Kingdom
Crabtree Publishing**
Maritime House
Basin Road North, Hove
BN41 1WR

**Published in Australia
Crabtree Publishing**
3 Charles Street
Coburg North
VIC, 3058

CONTENTS

YOU CAN BE AN ENTREPRENEUR!

In 2016, audio engineer Wake Anderson unveiled SoundBridge, a new type of digital audio workstation (DAW). It gave musicians the tools they need to produce high-quality recordings on their own. In the past, the only way to get a decent recording was to go to a studio, which cost a lot of money. Using SoundBridge was also a great way for beginner sound engineers to start practicing their trade.

Before SoundBridge, DAWs were often expensive or hard to use. **Amateurs** found it challenging to produce great recordings without help or financial backing. Anderson's **software** helped solve the problem. It was affordable and easy to use, and it didn't require any special equipment. Anderson is an example of an **entrepreneur**. He used his science and technology skills to develop a product that had the potential to change an entire **industry**, such as the music industry.

ENTREPRENEURS AND START-UPS

Entrepreneurs are people who come up with unique and **innovative** ideas. They think outside the box to come up with life-changing technologies and procedures. Entrepreneurs are willing to take risks by **investing** in new **goods** and **services**. They will do everything they can to be successful. Start-ups are new businesses that entrepreneurs start so they can promote and sell their ideas.

WHAT IS AN ENGINEER?

Engineers are people who design and build machines, structures, systems, and more. They use math and science to solve everyday problems. The main types of engineering are mechanical, chemical, **civil**, electrical, **marine**, and **aerospace**. There are hundreds of branches

A DAW is used to record, edit, mix, **compose**, and produce audio recordings.

of engineering within these main types. Engineers do everything from developing new types of plastic to designing space shuttles. Engineers can also be entrepreneurs, when they create businesses based on their ideas.

ENTREPRENEURS CHANGING THE WORLD

People around the world face many different challenges, such as natural disasters. Engineers find ways to solve these problems using their knowledge of science, technology, and math. Engineering entrepreneurs work in all types of industries, from construction to robotics. They look for new and innovative ideas to help make the world a better place. They may design buildings that can survive earthquakes, or find ways to get clean water to places where water is scarce.

Engineers can make a difference in people's lives. Some design pumps that provide clean water.

INSPIRING STORIES

Early Thinkers

Before the mid-1800s, the only way for people to communicate across long distances was by sending letters by mail. The invention of the **telegraph** changed all that, but it required long cables. A businessman named Cyrus Field created a start-up business to connect North America and Europe by cable. He asked British telegraph engineer Charles Tilston Bright to design a cable that would **transmit** telegraph signals across the ocean. The work Field and Bright did paved the way for fast, modern **telecommunications**.

Cyrus Field's company laid the first telegraph cable across the Atlantic Ocean.

AUDIO INNOVATIONS

Audio engineers are people who record, mix, and reproduce sounds. Thomas Edison was one of the first entrepreneurs in this field. In the late 1800s, he made the world's first recording of a musical performance. It lasted just 78 seconds and was made on a device called a **phonograph**. The sound quality was terrible, but it was a giant step forward for recording and playing sounds and music.

In 1878, Edison founded a start-up company and began selling the phonograph. It was the first device for recording and playing back sounds, and it changed the world. Over the next few decades, other audio entrepreneurs improved on Edison's design. They invented more advanced devices to record sounds, such as vinyl records.

Thomas Edison was just 30 years old when he invented the phonograph in 1877.

IMPROVING ON THE PAST

For nearly a century, audio recordings were captured on a **physical medium** that often sounded scratchy and wore out with use. In the 1960s, entrepreneurs started to look for ways to make **digital recordings**. These never wear out, and they always sound exactly the same as the original recording. **Compact discs (CDs)** were some of the first forms of digital recordings. Audio engineers kept looking for new and better ways to record sounds. Many, such as Wake Anderson, turned to the Internet and mobile devices to store, share, and create recordings.

Edison's phonograph recorded sounds on wax cylinders. Emile Berliner introduced flat discs, which worked better.

INSPIRING OTHERS

Audio engineers are forming start-ups to follow in the footsteps of Thomas Edison. A company called Pibox Music is making it easier for artists and engineers to **collaborate**. Pibox was cofounded by brothers Ivan and Pavel Talaychuk. They provide cloud-based file storage and the ability to use audio calls to share recordings. They also offer chat groups for individual projects and feedback tools for commenting on recordings.

Another start-up, Even, launched a product called EarPrint in 2016. Much like people take an eye test to get the right glasses, Even offers an online ear test to make sure they get the right headphones. EarPrint helps correct for differences in the way people hear to ensure they get the best sound every time.

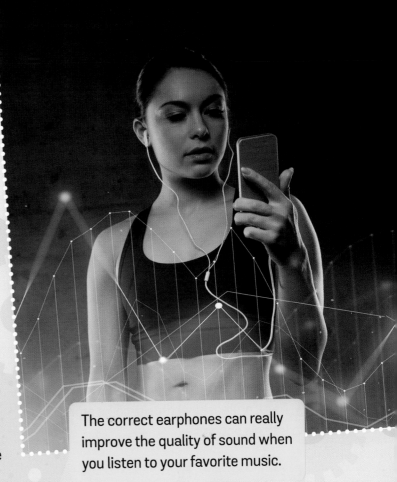

The correct earphones can really improve the quality of sound when you listen to your favorite music.

INSPIRING STORIES

Recording Music at Home

In the 1980s, UC Berkeley graduates Evan Brooks and Peter Gotcher created the world's first computer-based audio editing software, called Sound Tools. It allows users to change or improve sounds. Over time, Sound Tools became the popular DAW known as Pro Tools. People around the world use Pro Tools for sound recording and **production** projects.

Evan Brooks (below) and his cofounder Peter Gotcher were high school friends.

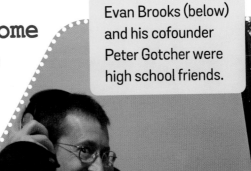

SOUND
START-UP STAR:
WAKE ANDERSON

George Wakefield "Wake" Anderson grew up studying **jazz** guitar in Portland, Maine. An avid musician, he was writing his own music by junior year in high school. By the time he was in college, he was recording and mixing his own music. He used the basic DAW that came with his computer. It wasn't long before Anderson outgrew the capabilities of the DAW he was using. He wanted to produce better quality, more professional music, so he started looking into his options.

To get the results he was after, Anderson would have to pay a lot of money for a high-end DAW. Instead, he began experimenting with free online software—but found it was very complicated to use. Anderson realized that musicians needed an easier way to record and share their creations. He started **mocking up** his own designs for what he thought would be the ultimate solution.

Anderson's company, SoundBridge, provides tools and features that are similar to the ones offered in professional recording studios.

ENTREPRENEUR FOR SOUND

Anderson graduated from Northeastern University with a Bachelor of Science degree in 2014. He then founded the start-up company SoundBridge. He began working with a team of artists and engineers to develop innovative new **audio engineering** software. Based in Boston, SoundBridge is an easy-to-use DAW that combines touchscreen technology with studio-quality gear. It can be used on desktop computers, mobile devices, and Internet browsers. It allows artists in different places to easily share data and collaborate with one another. Anderson states that his technology allows all types of musicians around the world to "record themselves from their bedroom."

SoundBridge partnered with SkyTracks to help artists collaborate within the DAW. A recording saved on the SkyTracks cloud can be accessed via the Internet.

AROUND THE WORLD

Anderson wants everyone in the world, from voice artists to amateur musicians, to have the tools they need to make great recordings. To support this vision, he decided to make SoundBridge available free of charge. To make money, the start-up company offers training programs and upgraded features for a fee.

POISED FOR SUCCESS

In 2016, SoundBridge was a MassChallenge Boston Awards finalist. The awards showcase the most promising entrepreneurs and start-ups from across the globe. In addition, SoundBridge was featured in the *Audiofanzine* article "Top 5 Most Innovative Products at The Winter NAMM Show 2016."

CONSTRUCTION COMPANIES

Before construction companies start work on a new project, such as a bridge, building, sewer system, or road, civil engineers need to create a plan for the project. Civil engineers are people who use science and math to design, construct, and maintain structures of all kinds. They look for ways to make them stronger, taller, longer-lasting, and more **efficient**.

In 1771, John Smeaton created the Society of Civil Engineers in Britain.

ENGINEERING PIONEER

In the mid-1700s, John Smeaton became the first person to call himself a civil engineer. Born in 1724 in Austhorpe, England, Smeaton took an early interest in science and engineering projects. By age 24, he started his own company and began designing mathematical instruments, including a **mariner's compass**. After years of scientific experiments, Smeaton began designing

bridges, canals, and harbors. His most famous civil engineering project was the Eddystone Lighthouse near Plymouth, England. He used innovative new techniques, such as interlocking **masonry** and fast-drying cement that would hold up underwater. His work provided inspiration for other civil engineering entrepreneurs.

PICTURE PERFECT

In 2014, Sam Lytle combined his love of video games and special effects with his expertise as a civil engineer. His start-up company, Civil FX, employs both artists and engineers. It uses computer software to create lifelike 3-D images and animations of construction projects, from bridges to buildings. It allows engineers, construction workers, and clients to see what a project will look like when it is complete.

Today, engineers in companies such as Civil FX use software to create highly realistic images of the constructions they plan to build.

CIVIL ENGINEERING TODAY

Forward-thinking civil engineers are using **carbon fiber** as a way to make structures stronger. Carbon fiber is five times stronger than steel, and twice as stiff. Entrepreneurs around the world are constantly inventing new ways of using carbon fiber. In 2013, Finnish elevator company KONE used carbon fiber to create KONE UltraRope. This rope is much lighter than regular steel cables. Since there is less weight to lift, an elevator's energy costs can be greatly reduced. Energy costs can go down by as much as 15 percent for an elevator that travels to a height of 1,640 feet (500 m). UltraRope can also raise elevators twice as high as traditional cables, which allows civil engineers to design taller skyscrapers.

KONE UltraRope will one day allow elevators to reach heights of 3,280 feet (1,000 m).

STEEL
START-UP STARS:
MICHAEL GRAY AND CARLOS DE OLIVEIRA

For many years, the strongest and most long-lasting building materials were not always easy to form into unique shapes and angles. But new technologies are changing this. Michael Gray was a civil engineering student at the University of Toronto when he began researching ways to use strong materials for unique designs. His solution was to build structures by pouring liquid steel into a mold and letting it cool. Different molds would allow engineers to design beautiful structures that were also strong and long-lasting.

Gray's groundbreaking work using this product, called cast steel, won many important awards. It led him to create a start-up company with fellow civil engineer Carlos de Oliveira. Founded in 2007, CAST CONNEX makes cast-steel parts for construction projects.

Michael Gray (below) formed a start-up with Carlos de Oliveira (left). Their products have helped revolutionize construction work in earthquake-prone places.

SUPER-STRONG STEEL

A big part of civil engineering is finding new ways to make buildings stronger and safer. Many factors, such as natural disasters, can affect a structure's ability to continue standing over a long period of time. During their university studies, Gray and de Oliveira spent a great deal of time researching ways to build earthquake-**resistant** structures. In 2006, they came up with a solution—special cast-steel connectors, which would strengthen the steel tubing that makes up a structure's **frame**.

Hundreds of thousands of people died in the 7.0 **magnitude** earthquake that shook Haiti in January 2010.

Following a devastating earthquake in Haiti in 2010, the company donated its connectors to rebuild École Lakay. This school is near the capital city of Port-au-Prince. Now that it can withstand earthquakes, the school will also act as a shelter where locals can get food and medical care in the event of future disasters. Since then, CAST CONNEX has become an industry leader in developing products for areas that have a lot of earthquakes. The company's cast-steel **nodes** are an important part of the massive Transbay Transit Center (TTC). This transit station is in San Francisco, where earthquakes are common.

The TTC in San Francisco is a public transportation hub that will also feature stores and restaurants. Construction began on it in 2010.

BEAUTIFUL BUILDINGS

Traditional steel construction involves **welding** large steel plates together. Cast steel is very **flexible** and can take on any shape and size. It can even be hollow. CAST CONNEX is one of the first companies to use cast steel for structural engineering projects. One of the best features of cast steel is that it can be used to create unique shapes and angles. Designers can come up with creative ideas, and CAST CONNEX makes them possible to build.

ENVIRONMENTAL AWARENESS

Did you know that more than two billion people around the world do not have access to clean water? People need clean water to drink, grow food, cook, bathe, and more. Without it, they are at risk of disease or even death. The lack of access to clean water is just one of many environmental issues that have an impact on people every day. Air **pollution** is another example. This kind of pollution can contribute to **global warming**.

To combat environmental issues, people need to find sustainable ways to manage Earth's **resources** and protect public health. Environmental engineers use their knowledge of soil science, chemistry, and biology to find solutions to environmental issues. From recycling programs to treating, or cleaning, polluted water, environmental engineers work to protect the environment.

Ward's Island Wastewater Treatment Plant provides clean water to the residents of New York City.

STINKY SOLUTION

In the mid–1800s, sewage in London, England, drained into the Thames River. This quickly became a problem because people got their drinking water from the Thames. It wasn't long before a disease called **cholera** began to spread. On top of that, the stench from the river was so bad that the government offered a huge reward for a solution. Joseph Bazalgette designed an **elaborate** sewage system for the city. His solution kept water clean and stopped the spread of

Today, Joseph Bazalgette is remembered as the world's first environmental engineer.

WATER WISE

In many cities today, aging sewers and pipes cannot keep up with the demands of growing communities. In 2016, entrepreneur Thouheed Abdul Gaffoor found a way to help solve this problem. While studying environmental engineering, Gaffoor cofounded EMAGIN. This start-up company uses **artificial intelligence** to help communities manage their water systems. EMAGIN's software monitors water systems for problems and tracks daily demand.

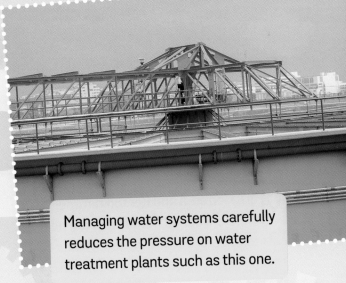

Managing water systems carefully reduces the pressure on water treatment plants such as this one.

Gray Water Recycling

Dirty water from doing laundry or washing the dishes is called gray water. In many places, it runs down the drain and is carried to a water treatment facility. There, it is filtered before being released into a river. But what if there was an easy way to clean and reuse this water for tasks such as watering the garden or flushing the toilet? In places such as California, where **droughts** are common, reusing gray water is extremely important. Australian engineer Tom Wood has found a way to capture gray water for reuse. His start-up company, Nexus eWater, produced the world's first in-home water and energy recycling system. It can recycle as much as 67 percent of water used indoors. In California, homeowners and builders, as well as energy companies, are already using Nexus eWater to recycle gray water.

Tom Wood's system doesn't just recycle — it can also use gray water to create heat energy.

PLASTIC
START-UP STARS:
MARK HERREMA AND KENTON KIMMEL

Mark Herrema and Kenton Kimmel were childhood friends and are now entrepreneurs. They were determined to find a positive way to capture and use the carbon that goes into the air. In 2003, while Mark was studying at Princeton University and Kenton at Northwestern University, they created a small company called Newlight Technologies and began to search for a solution.

Herrema graduated with a degree in politics and Kimmel with a degree in biomedical engineering. The two friends then continued their scientific research. They took jobs at a hotel to help fund their start-up company and spent their free time working on their research. Finally, in 2010, they hit a breakthrough. "Waking up the next morning felt like Christmas," Herrema remembers.

Oil **refineries**, such as the one below, produce a great deal of carbon that goes into the air.

Evan Creelman (left) joined Mark Herrema (center) and Kenton Kimmel (right) as part of the Newlight Technologies team.

CAPTURING CARBON

Carbon is an important part of Earth's **atmosphere**. It is found inside all living things, such as plants and animals, as well as inside rocks, soil, and **fossil fuels** such as oil and coal. When carbon is released, it becomes **carbon dioxide**. Too much carbon dioxide is a problem.

For a long time, people have been mining and burning fossil fuels to heat homes, run cars, power factories, and light buildings. This releases carbon dioxide much more quickly than normal. The result is global warming, which makes glaciers melt, forests die off, and rivers and lakes dry up. One way to stop global warming is through carbon capture. As much as 90 percent of carbon dioxide can be captured so it isn't released into the atmosphere. Environmental engineers are always looking for ways to capture carbon.

Most often, they capture it at its source of emission and transport it to massive underground storage lockers. Herrema and Kimmel used carbon-capture technology to create AirCarbon.

AIRCARBON AWARENESS

Herrema and Kimmel take carbon that would otherwise go into the air and use it to make AirCarbon. This biodegradable material is an environmentally friendly product. It behaves similarly to regular plastics, but costs less to produce. Companies such as Dell and L'Oreal are commercializing AirCarbon to make products such as packaging, chairs, and containers. In many ways, AirCarbon is a win-win: It keeps carbon out of the atmosphere and creates useful products. In 2014, Newlight was named one of 24 "Technology **Pioneers**" by the World Economic Forum.

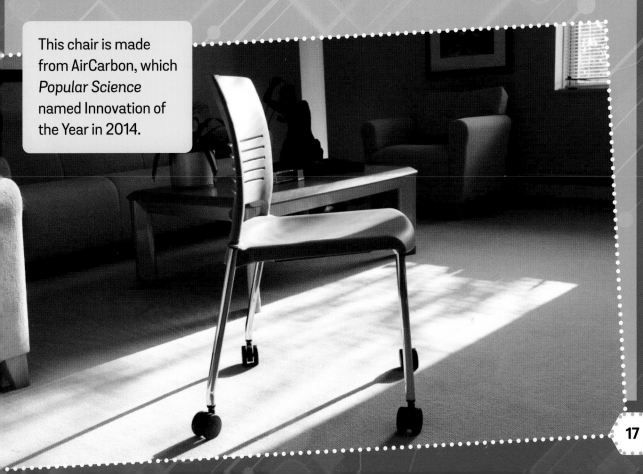

This chair is made from AirCarbon, which *Popular Science* named Innovation of the Year in 2014.

RADICAL ROBOTICS

Have you ever seen a robot vacuum cleaner spinning around a room? Robots are machines that are used to perform jobs. They can do simple jobs, such as cleaning a floor, or more complex jobs, such as building cars or performing surgeries. Sometimes, robots do the work on their own. Other times, people control the work that robots do.

Robotics engineers are people who design and build robots. They also design software and processes to run robots. They think about every movement, action, and activity a robot needs to perform a certain task and come up with ways to make them happen.

TWENTIETH-CENTURY TELEVOX

In 1923, Roy Wensley, an engineer with Westinghouse Electric and **Manufacturing** Company, unveiled a remote control system that became the technology that created the world's first robot four years later. Known as Herbert Televox, the robot could answer a phone call, operate switches, and wave its arms.

Herbert Televox was a cardboard cutout character placed in front of a Televox system.

Robot vacuum cleaners are common in many homes across North America.

SOPHISTICATED SYSTEMS

With the invention of the digital computer, engineers started thinking about building robots with computer brains. General Motors released the first programmable robot in 1961. It could move hot metal objects from one place to another. Within five years, inventors at Stanford Research Institute (SRI) developed a robot that used artificial intelligence to make decisions about how to perform tasks.

In 2017, robotics engineer Pieter Abbeel cofounded Embodied Intelligence. This start-up company is using artificial intelligence and virtual reality to teach robots how to act like humans. Using virtual reality headsets and handheld motion trackers, human movements are recreated in a digital environment. A robot observes the movements and mimics them. Embodied Intelligence plans to start by teaching robots how to move wires and cables. Then they will learn more complex tasks.

Virtual reality headsets allow people to "teach" robots how to act like humans. The robots copy their movements and behavior.

INSPIRING STORIES

Robots in Extreme Locations

Today, robots perform all kinds of jobs. Some even work in space or underwater. The Canadarm2 is a robotic arm used as part of the **International Space Station (ISS)**. It is used to move around supplies, equipment, and astronauts. OceanOne is a "robo mermaid" built by Stanford University science professor Oussama Khatib. A pilot uses joysticks to control the underwater robot, which can perform many of the same tasks as a human diver. OceanOne has special sensors that allow the pilot to see everything the robot sees, and feel anything it touches.

OceanOne can explore in places that are too dangerous for human divers.

ROBOT
START-UP STAR:
RODOLPHE HASSELVANDER

For years, people have been dreaming of robots that can help with daily tasks or be their best friends. Until recently, that dream was still a long way off. Engineer Rodolphe Hasselvander is the cofounder and **CEO** of the start-up company Blue Frog Robotics. He had a dream of having a robot companion from a very young age.

In 2001, Hasselvander began working as an engineer for a French car maker that produces brands such as Peugeot and Citroën. Three years later, he became the youngest person to lead research and development at CRIIF—a robotics association in France. After 13 years working with top robotics researchers, Hasselvander created Blue Frog Robotics in 2014. "We want to put a robot in every home," he said.

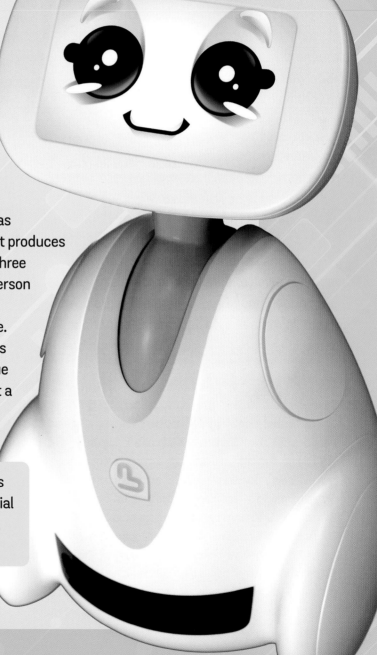

Buddy is one of Hasselvander's inventions. The robot has special software that allows it to hear, speak, and see.

YOUR NEW BEST FRIEND

In 2015, Blue Frog unveiled Buddy. This family-friendly robot has a cute face and the ability to help around the house with basic tasks. The companion robot has a huge personality, and uses different facial expressions to interact with its family. With Buddy, Hasselvander had met his goal of creating a friendly robot with accessible, user-friendly technology.

Blue Frog gave Buddy big eyes, a large head, and a short, thick body so it would look like a human baby. Buddy is nearly 2 feet tall (61 cm) and weighs just 13 pounds (6 kg). It moves around on three wheels and has a tablet for a brain. Buddy can play games, connect to smartphones and **social networks**, play music and videos, and sense security issues in a home. It can schedule events, create to-do lists, search for recipes, provide weather reports, and much more. Hasselvander would like to see Buddy used as a hub for all sorts of smart objects and devices in the home. Smart lights, appliances, and switches are just a few examples.

Buddy was created using open-source software. Open-source means that the technology is available to anyone. It allows robotics engineers and software developers around the world to help design new features for Buddy. In fact, shortly after Buddy made his debut, he received a facelift. He was given all new facial expressions, so that he can show a full range of emotions, from happy to sad. Buddy is also equipped with 3-D vision that allows him to tell the difference among an object, a plant, an animal, and a person.

Rodolphe Hasselvander aims to develop more robots like Buddy that will make life easier for people and help them have fun.

TAKING FLIGHT

The Montgolfier brothers' balloon soared 3,000 feet (915 m) above the ground, traveling nearly 6 miles (10 km) in 25 minutes.

On November 21, 1783, humans flew for the first time. It happened in a hot-air balloon invented by French brothers Joseph-Michel and Jacques-Étienne Montgolfier. It wasn't long before other inventors began looking for ways to mimic the brothers' success.

Later, Wilbur and Orville Wright made the first powered flight in an airplane, later selling their planes to the U.S. Army. The even farther-reaching **Soviet** engineer Sergey Korolyov designed the first rocket capable of launching into space in 1957. These engineers and entrepreneurs paved the way for modern aerospace engineers.

AEROSPACE ENGINEERING

People who build and design flying machines are called aerospace engineers. There are two types of aerospace engineers. Aeronautical engineers focus on machines that fly within Earth's atmosphere, such as airplanes and helicopters. Astronautical engineers work on machines that fly into space, such as **satellites** and spacecraft with human crews.

Space in airplanes can be used flexibly with the Butterfly seating system. It allows passengers to work, relax, or sleep on board as needed.

THE SKY'S THE LIMIT

Since the Wright brothers' first flight, there have been incredible advances in aeronautics, from in-flight refueling to planes that take off and land vertically. Some aeronautics engineers even use their skills to redesign outdated systems. For example, Hong Kong–based engineer and entrepreneur James Lee launched a start-up company called Paperclip Design Limited in 2012. Often, airplanes have lots of empty first-class seats, while their economy seats are overbooked. Lee developed a unique seating system called Butterfly. It allows flight crews to convert first-class seats into economy seats, as needed. This lets airlines make the most use of the space on their planes.

SPACE RACE

Aerospace engineers look beyond Earth's atmosphere. Deep Space Industries (DSI) was founded in 2013 with the goal of mining resources from asteroids. The company plans to extract water and precious metals and sell them on Earth or to other companies that are doing work in space. While it will still be a long time before they are ready to harvest resources in space, DSI is currently working on advanced spacecraft, satellites, and robots that can do the work when the time comes. It has built two spacecraft and has applied for a **patent** for its innovative **microgravity** manufacturing technology.

In the future, satellites will send us data about the resources in space. We can then collect and use the resources on Earth.

AEROSPACE
START-UP STAR:
SUSMITA MOHANTY

Aerospace engineer Susmita Mohanty's love of space grew from an early age. Her father was part of India's space program, and she dreamed of following in his footsteps. She was fascinated with the idea of "space architecture"—habitats, products, and transportation systems that could be used for exploring space.

Mohanty earned a Bachelor's degree in electrical engineering and a Master's degree in industrial design in India. After that, she wanted to study at the International Space University (ISU) in Strasbourg, France, but the program cost $35,000. So she wrote letters to people such as Bill Gates and Carl Sagan to ask them to help pay for her studies.

Finally, Arthur C. Clarke—author of the science-fiction classic *2001: A Space Odyssey*—paid for her studies. He also became her mentor. Following her space studies at ISU, Mohanty got her **doctorate** in aerospace architecture.

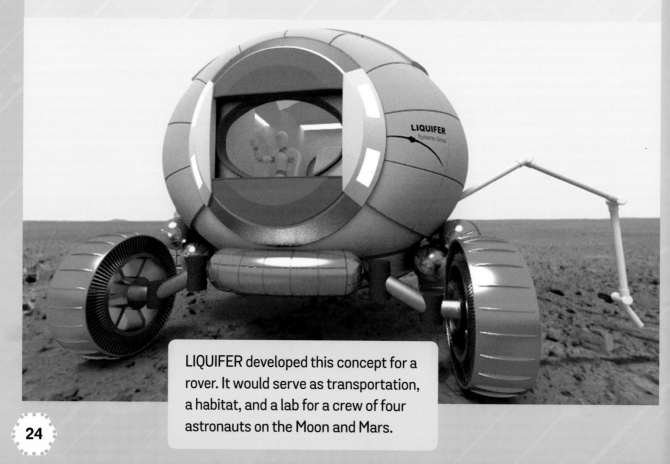

LIQUIFER developed this concept for a rover. It would serve as transportation, a habitat, and a lab for a crew of four astronauts on the Moon and Mars.

BRANCHING OUT

Mohanty started her space career by working at aircraft manufacturing company Boeing and at NASA's Space Center. In 2001, at age 29, she founded her first start-up company—a space consulting firm called MoonFront. Consulting firms have one or more experts who can offer professional advice about a certain topic.

Two years later, she started the company LIQUIFER to design ideas for traveling and living in space. The company is made up of **architects**, industrial designers, engineers, and scientists. They design future human and robotics systems for space exploration and habitats. They use cutting-edge ideas and technologies to work on a variety of space-related research and development projects.

SPACE VENTURES

In 2008, Mohanty moved back to India and launched the space start-up Earth2Orbit. The company's goal is to help India become a world leader in the use and exploration of space. Mohanty now works on projects related to lunar and Mars exploration, and launching satellites on Indian rockets.

In 2017, Mohanty introduced a new idea called Earth2Orbit Analytix. It uses data from Earth-observation satellites to look for ways to help businesses and communities. The company uses satellite images to provide information. This data helps organizations save money and help the environment in their area. The data is especially useful for farming, insurance, environment, and **infrastructure** companies.

AWARD-WINNING ENTREPRENEUR

Nicknamed "The Moon Walker," Mohanty has received many honors for her work as an entrepreneur. She won the Women in Aerospace (WIA) International Achievement Award and was included on the *Financial Times'* "25 Indians to Watch" list.

Mohanty stands under the nozzle of an Ariane rocket at the 2017 Paris Air Show. The event showcases innovations in aerospace technology.

ENTREPRENEURS CHANGING THE WORLD

As people learn more and more about the world around them, they also learn more about science and technology and how they can be used to improve life for everyone on Earth. Engineers are people who use science, technology, and math to design, build, and maintain systems and structures. One of their main goals is to solve problems. Whatever their field of work, engineers share a common goal: improving existing inventions or making new ones. Whether they're looking for ways to reduce pollution or explore space, engineers help make the world a better place.

Some engineers look for ways to design stronger, more efficient structures, such as bridges and towers. Others focus on inventing robots that can do dangerous jobs so that humans don't have to. Other engineers search for ways to make it possible for people to travel beyond Earth's atmosphere. Engineers such as Wake Anderson make creating music accessible for all people. Even more engineers, such as the men behind Newlight Technologies, make Earth a better place to live by protecting the environment.

Robots are becoming more common. It is estimated that one in 10 homes in the United States will have a robot by 2020.

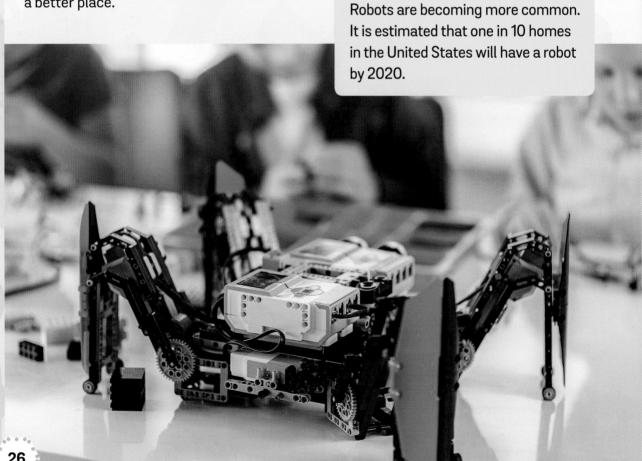

TAKING RISKS

Entrepreneurs are people who are willing to
take risks in starting a business. They invest
in bringing ideas to life. Early inventors such
as Thomas Edison, who dreamed of better
ways of communicating, were entrepreneurs.
Their work made it possible for modern-day
entrepreneurs such as Wake Anderson and
Susmita Mohanty to create and innovate.
Many engineers become entrepreneurs when
they turn their innovations into businesses.

ENGINEERING IS THE FUTURE

Think of the challenges early engineers
faced. They did not have some of the
scientific knowledge and innovative tools
engineers have today. Yet, they embraced
these challenges to come up with new ideas.
What problems will we face in the future
that engineers will have to solve? Will there
be new ways to get clean water to people all
around the world? Will there be civilizations
in space? Will robots be doing
our laundry? Engineering
entrepreneurs are designing
and building new systems
and structures all the time.
Perhaps one day, you will be
one of those entrepreneurs!

Engineering camps give
students the chance to explore
different types of engineering,
such as robotics.

YOUR START-UP STORY

Engineers are changing the world with their innovative approaches to building and designing systems and structures. Engineering entrepreneurs work in all types of industries, and their ideas are shaped by the many challenges people face each day.

TAKE THE START-UP CHALLENGE!

Around the world, people face many challenges, such as lack of clean water. Engineers and entrepreneurs are working to solve these problems. For example, some entrepreneurial engineers are developing systems and structures for **filtering** and delivering clean water in places that require it. What ideas can you come up with as an entrepreneur to address this issue?

As an entrepreneur, it's important to have an idea that others will find useful and affordable. It should solve a problem that people face often. Do research to find out if other entrepreneurs are working on solving the same problem. How is your solution different? Does it cost less, or is it easier to produce? If there is nothing else like it out there, think about why that might be. Is there a demand, or a need, for it? Once you have found a unique solution to a problem and know that people want it, you're ready to start designing it. Try the activity on the next page to kickstart your career as an entrepreneur!

Engineers look for ways to get clean water to communities such as Lilongwe, Malawi. There, many people get their water from a single tap.

BUILD A WATER FILTRATION SYSTEM

Imagine you are an environmental engineer who needs to provide a way of cleaning contaminated water. You have decided the best solution is to filter the dirty water.

You Will Need
- A plastic jug of dirty water (use soil and sand)
- A clear plastic cup of clean water
- Filter materials: coffee filters, cotton balls, mesh, grass, paper towels, tissues, gauze pads
- Three clear plastic cups
- Paper
- Pen

Instructions
Use the materials to design three different filters. You can use more than one item per filter. Put each of the filters on top of a clear plastic cup, then pour some of the dirty water through each filter. Compare the water in each cup to clean water. Which filter worked best?

To succeed, a business must make money. Calculate the cost of producing each of your filters by adding up the cost of the materials you used. Use the following values:

Coffee filters	$3 each
Cotton balls	$2 each
Mesh	$1 each
Grass	$0.25 per handful
Paper towels	$0.75 each
Tissues	$0.50 each
Gauze pads	$1 each

Was the most effective filter also the cheapest? If not, could you redesign it using cheaper materials, but without losing any of its effectiveness?

Water fountains provide clean drinking water, but not everyone has access to them.

GLOSSARY

aerospace A branch of science and technology related to building machines that fly

amateurs People who practice in a field of work but are not paid to do so

architects People who design buildings and oversee their construction

artificial intelligence The use of computers to do tasks that require human intelligence

atmosphere Blanket of gases that surrounds Earth and some other planets

audio engineering Working with the technical parts of recording, editing, and mixing sounds

carbon dioxide A gas found in the air that can cause global warming when it builds up in the atmosphere and traps the Sun's heat

carbon fiber Very thin strand of carbon

CEO (short for **Chief Executive Officer**) A person who is in charge of a company

cholera A disease in the small intestine caused by drinking contaminated water

civil Relating to people and their concerns

collaborate To work with a group of people

compact discs (CDs) Small plastic discs used to record and store sounds, such as music

compose To write or create

digital recordings Sound waves that are converted into a pattern of numbers

doctorate The highest degree at a university

droughts Periods of low rainfall

efficient Achieving something using less energy or by doing less work

elaborate Very detailed and impressive

entrepreneur A person who creates a business and takes on most of the risk to operate it

filtering Removing substances from a liquid

flexible Able to bend or be bent

fossil fuels Natural fuels formed long ago from dead plants and animals

frame A solid structure that acts as a support for a building and all of its parts

global warming The gradual increase of Earth's temperature

goods Products; something made

industry Business activity related to the manufacture of goods and provision of services

infrastructure The systems and services that act as the foundation for a community, such as roads, utilities, and structures

innovative Describing something that no one else has done before

International Space Station (ISS) A large satellite built to house people in space

investing Giving money to help start up a company in exchange for owning part of that company

jazz A type of music that originated in the United States in the early 1900s

magnitude Size; a measurement of the force of an earthquake

manufacturing The process of making goods to sell

marine To do with oceans and seas

mariner's compass A navigation tool that shows direction

masonry Stonework

microgravity When gravity is so weak that objects appear weightless

mocking up Making a full-size model of something for testing

nodes Connecting points

patent A government license giving a person or company the sole right to sell, use, or make an invention

phonograph A device that produces sound through the vibration of a needle following a groove on a spinning disc

physical medium An object on which sounds, words, or images are recorded

pioneers People who are the first to use or develop something

pollution The presence of harmful substances in the environment

production The act of making or manufacturing something

refineries Industrial plants that have the buildings and equipment to process substances such as oil

resistant Offering protection or resistance against something

resources A supply of materials or other assets that can be used

satellites Artificial objects that are sent into orbit around a planet or other body in space

services Types of help or work that someone does for someone else

social networks Websites and applications that allow people to communicate with each other online

software Programs that computers use to operate

Soviet Someone or something associated with the former Soviet Union, which has now split into Russia and several smaller countries

telecommunications Communications that occur over a long distance

telegraph A method of sending and receiving messages through electrical or radio signals

transmit To send something out or pass it from one place to another

welding Joining metal parts together by heating them until they begin to melt, then pressing them together

LEARNING MORE

BOOKS

Hynson, Colin. *Dream Jobs in Engineering*. Crabtree Publishing Company, 2017.

Kopp, Megan. *Space Tech: High-tech Space Science*. Crabtree Publishing Company, 2017.

Lundgren, Julie. *STEM Jobs with the Environment*. Rourke Publishing Group, 2014.

Rooney, Anne. *Audio Engineering and the Science of Sound Waves*. Crabtree Publishing Company, 2014.

Sutherland, Adam. *Be a Young Entrepreneur: Get Inspired to Be a Business Whiz*. Barron's Educational Series, 2016.

WEBSITES

Biz Kids
This website offers lots of great information about how to start and run a business.
http://bizkids.com

Kidpreneurs
Learn more about young entrepreneurs and their inspiring stories.
http://kidpreneurs.org/blog

Try Engineering
Find out more about what engineering is and why it's important.
http://tryengineering.org

INDEX

ABOUT THE AUTHOR

Heather C. Hudak has written hundreds of books for children and edited thousands more. She loves traveling the world, learning about new cultures, and spending time with her husband and many pets.